# LAUNCHPAD

A Real-World Guide to Internships and Entry-Level Success

KAYDIAN WILLIAMS

ISBN: 978-1-966723-36-3 (paperback)

# DEDICATION

To every student I've had the privilege of guiding, and to those I may never meet but still hope to inspire, this is for you.

May you step boldly into new spaces, carry your confidence like a compass, and remember that your voice belongs in every room you enter.

# ACKNOWLEDGEMENT

This book is born out of the countless conversations, questions, and dreams I've shared with students over the years.

To those who trusted me with your stories and aspirations, thank you for reminding me why this work matters. I am deeply grateful to my mentors and peers in the field of human resources, who have modeled integrity, wisdom, and resilience. Your example continues to shape how I encourage the next generation.

To my family, your unwavering support has been my anchor. Every word written is rooted in your belief in me.

And finally, to every young professional stepping into the unknown, your courage is the spark behind this book. My hope is that these pages will meet you right where you are and help you launch toward where you're meant to be.

# TABLE OF CONTENTS

# INTRODUCTION

Transitioning from college to the workforce can feel like preparing for liftoff.

Whether you're landing an internship at a startup or starting your first job at a Fortune 500 company, this book is designed to guide you clearly, practically, and with a voice that speaks directly to your real-world challenges. In these pages, you'll discover insights that matter now, not outdated advice that worked ten years ago. You'll learn to navigate remote meetings, understand corporate culture, speak up in virtual meetings, and show up in a way that gets noticed for the right reasons.

This is your playbook for confidence, clarity, and career momentum.

Let's take off!

# CHAPTER 1
# YOUR LAUNCH BEGINS NOW

This is it! The beginning of your professional journey. Whether you're gearing up for your very first internship or walking into your first official entry-level role, this moment marks your personal launch, and like any launch, it matters how you prepare, how you approach it, and how you navigate the unknowns ahead.

Internships and early roles aren't just stepping stones, they're rocket fuel. These experiences are designed to expose you to real-world work, team dynamics, deadlines, and the professional expectations that differ from academic life. They're not just about fetching coffee or shadowing someone with a title; they're about contribution, growth, and forming the foundation of your career identity. They allow you to experiment with your talents, find out what you enjoy (or don't), and build relationships that could shape the direction of your future. The mindset you carry into this stage of your life sets the tone for everything else. It influences your reputation, resilience, and even your confidence in taking on leadership later.

This is where your habits start to solidify how you show up, how you learn, how you bounce back, and how you stretch yourself. This phase is your proving ground, not because you need to be perfect, but because you need to be present. Fully present! Absorbing what you see, applying what you've learned, and aligning with who you're becoming. Think of it this way: *"How you approach your first 100 days in the working world can define your trajectory for the next 1,000."* Gone are the days when you were expected to walk into a cubicle at 9 a.m. and leave at 5 p.m. Today's work world is more complex, dynamic, and flexible than ever before. Interns and entry-level professionals are entering environments that may be hybrid, remote, or on-site. Each of these models comes with unique expectations, tools, and communication styles. Knowing how to adapt to each and understanding the nuances of how work gets done in different formats are a critical skill in today's job market.

You might attend your first team online meeting while sitting at your kitchen table, build connections with coworkers you've never met in person, or you may navigate an open-office workspace with collaboration happening at every turn. No matter the setting, the ability to adapt and thrive is your new superpower.

In this book, you'll find practical tools, real-world examples, and thought-provoking prompts to help you succeed. Whether you're walking into a buzzing office downtown, logging into a Slack channel, holding a virtual meeting from your bedroom, or splitting time between both worlds, this is your launchpad.

Let's get you ready to take off!

# CHAPTER 2
# PREPARING FOR TAKEOFF SELF-ASSESSMENT AND GOAL SETTING

Before you can confidently launch into your internship or first job, it's essential to take a moment to pause. Preparation isn't just about crafting a resume or applying to positions; it starts with a deep and honest self-assessment. Understanding who you are, what you want, and where you're headed creates a solid foundation that will guide every decision, action, and interaction during your early career.

Self-assessment means more than just listing your skills or checking off achievements. It involves reflecting on your strengths, the qualities and abilities that energize you and bring out your best work. It also means acknowledging your weaknesses or areas for growth without judgment, recognizing that these are opportunities waiting to be developed.

*What kind of work excites you? What drains your energy? What values are non-negotiable in your professional life?*

This introspection will help you set clear, meaningful goals. Goals aren't just lofty ambitions; they're practical guides that steer your daily choices. Instead of vague resolutions like "do well" or "learn a lot," effective goals are specific, measurable, achievable, relevant, and time-bound (SMART). For example, "Improve my Excel skills by completing an online course within the next two months," or "Build relationships with at least three colleagues across different departments during my internship."

The act of goal setting serves a powerful purpose: it turns intentions into commitments. When you write down your goals, you're more likely to follow through. They help you prioritize your time and energy, giving your days direction and purpose. Goals also provide motivation when the inevitable challenges arise, reminding you why you started and what you're working toward. But setting goals isn't a one-time task. It's a dynamic process that requires regular check-ins and adjustments. As you gain experience and learn more about yourself and your workplace, your goals will evolve. Maybe you discover a passion for a particular aspect of your internship you hadn't considered before, or you realize certain skills need more attention. Being flexible and reflective will keep you growing in the right direction.

An honest self-assessment paired with thoughtful goal setting also helps you communicate clearly with supervisors and mentors. When asked about your development needs or career aspirations, you'll be ready with specific answers that show insight and initiative. This clarity makes it easier for others to support you, provide meaningful feedback, and connect you with opportunities that fit your path. Finally, remember that preparation isn't about perfection. No one starts their career with all the answers. What matters most is your willingness to understand yourself, set purposeful goals, and embrace the journey ahead with curiosity and resilience. This mindset will not only make you ready to take off, but also ready to soar.

# CHAPTER 3
# RESUME, COVER LETTER, AND LINKEDIN OPTIMIZATION

In today's hyper-competitive job market, your resume, cover letter, and LinkedIn profile are more than just documents; they are your digital handshake, your brand statement, and your first impression before you ever set foot into an interview. This chapter guides you through the process of strategically crafting each of these tools to stand out with clarity and confidence. Your resume isn't just a list of what you've done, it's proof of what you're capable of. I explore how to shift from simply listing duties to highlighting results. Using action verbs, measurable achievements, and tailored keywords, your resume should quickly tell a recruiter why you're the right fit. I also break down the difference between a general resume and one tailored to specific roles or industries, especially when applying to internships or entry-level roles in different sectors.

The cover letter? It's your opportunity to tell a short, compelling story. I guide you through how to write one that's both professional and personal, focusing not only on your qualifications but also on your curiosity, passion, and cultural fit. Rather than repeating your resume, the cover letter connects the dots and explains why you're applying to this company for this role at this time.

LinkedIn has become your online resume, networking hub, and credibility tracker all in one. This chapter teaches you how to optimize your headline, summary, and experience sections with authenticity and searchability. I also cover how to build your network, engage with content, and showcase skills and endorsements that position you as proactive and professional, even as a student or recent grad.

Each element of your career toolkit, your resume, cover letter, and LinkedIn profile, tells part of your story. Together, they should present a cohesive, confident picture of who you are and where you're headed. Crafting your resume, cover letter, and LinkedIn profile is your first opportunity to make a strong impression in the professional world. These three components form the foundation of your personal brand: how you present your skills, experiences, and potential to employers, recruiters, and professional connections. Getting them right is crucial to standing out, whether you're applying to a small company, a large corporation, or a Fortune 500 organization.

## RESUME: YOUR PERSONAL MARKETING DOCUMENT

Your resume is a concise summary of your education, experience, skills, and accomplishments. It's often the very first thing recruiters and hiring managers see, so it must be clear, focused, and tailored to each opportunity. Below, you will find a few tips to help you craft your resume.

## KEY TIPS FOR CRAFTING YOUR RESUME

- **Keep It Focused and Relevant**

As a student or recent graduate, your resume won't be long, and that's okay. Highlight internships, volunteer work, projects, relevant coursework, and part-time jobs that demonstrate transferable skills such as teamwork, problem-solving, and communication. Avoid including unrelated or outdated jobs, unless they highlight important skills.

- **Quantify Your Achievements**

Numbers stand out and make your contributions tangible. Instead of saying, "Helped with social media," say "Increased social media engagement by 20% over three months." Even small wins show impact.

- **Use Action Verbs**

Start bullet points with strong verbs like "led," "developed," "organized," or "analyzed." This communicates initiative and leadership.

- **Tailor for Each Job**

Use keywords from the internship or job description and adjust your resume to emphasize the skills and experiences that best align with the role. Applicant tracking systems (ATS) used by larger companies often scan for these keywords, so tailoring your application is crucial.

- **Keep Formatting Simple and Professional**

Use clear fonts, consistent spacing, and avoid excessive graphics or colors, unless you're applying for a creative role where such elements are expected.

## COVER LETTER: YOUR STORY AND WHY YOU FIT

While your resume provides a factual overview, your cover letter is your opportunity to tell a story, explaining why you want the position, how your background prepares you for it, and what you bring to the team. Many applicants skip this step or write generic letters; however, a tailored, thoughtful cover letter can make a significant difference.

## HOW TO WRITE AN EFFECTIVE COVER LETTER

- **Start Strong**

Address the letter to the hiring manager whenever possible and begin with a compelling opening sentence that grabs attention and expresses enthusiasm for the role and company.

- **Explain Your "Why"**

Why this company? Why this role? Explain your motivation and passion. Companies want to hire candidates who are genuinely interested and aligned with their mission, so it's important to know your "why."

- **Highlight Relevant Experience**

Don't repeat your resume word-for-word. Instead, pick one or two examples that showcase how your skills and achievements relate to the job's needs.

- **Show What You Offer**

Explain how you can contribute value. This could be your fresh perspective, technical skills, or strong work ethic.

- **Keep It Concise**

Aim for one page or less. Be clear and focused.

## PROOFREAD

Typos or errors can signal a lack of attention to detail. Read your letter aloud or ask a mentor or friend to review it on your behalf.

## LINKEDIN: YOUR PROFESSIONAL ONLINE PRESENCE

In today's digital-first hiring world, LinkedIn is more important than ever. It's a platform for networking, research, and showcasing your professional identity. Recruiters use LinkedIn to find candidates, and hiring managers often review profiles before interviews.

## OPTIMIZING YOUR LINKEDIN PROFILE

- **Professional Photo**

Use a clear, friendly headshot with a neutral background, and avoid casual or party pictures.

- **Compelling Headline**

Instead of just your student status, use your headline to communicate what you're studying and what kind of opportunities you seek, for example, "Marketing Student | Aspiring Digital Strategist | Content Creator."

- **Custom URL**

Customize your LinkedIn URL (linkedin.com/in/your name) to make it easier to share and more professional.

- **Detailed Summary**

Write a first-person summary that highlights your background, skills, passions, and career goals. Use this space to tell your story and invite connections.

- **Experience and Education**

Include details about your relevant internships, jobs, projects, and education. Use bullet points to highlight achievements, similar to those on your resume.

- **Skills and Endorsements**

Add skills relevant to your field and seek endorsements from professors, colleagues, or mentors.

- **Recommendations**

Ask for thoughtful LinkedIn recommendations that speak to your character and work ethic.

- **Engage and Network**

Share articles, comment on posts, join groups, and connect with people in your industry. Being active on LinkedIn increases your visibility.

## HOW TO APPROACH THESE DOCUMENTS STRATEGICALLY

- **Start Early and Revise Often**

Don't wait until the last minute to prepare these materials. Start early, gather feedback from mentors, career centers, or peers, and update your progress regularly.

- **Be Authentic**

Don't exaggerate or fabricate; authenticity builds trust.

- **Leverage Resources**

Many universities offer resume workshops, mock interviews, and LinkedIn training. Use these!

## CONSIDER YOUR AUDIENCE

A startup may value creativity and adaptability, so a slightly more dynamic resume may be beneficial. A large corporation might prefer a clean, traditional format, as tailoring is key. By carefully crafting your resume, cover letter, and LinkedIn profile, you create a powerful launchpad that opens doors to your first internship and beyond. These tools communicate not just what you've done, but who you are, your potential, professionalism, and passion. Nail these foundations, and you'll stand out as a confident, prepared, and capable candidate ready to take on the working world.

## NAILING THE INTERVIEW (AND WHAT TO DO AFTER)

The interview is your opportunity to bring your resume to life, showing not just what you've done, but who you are, how you think, and how you'll contribute. Whether it's virtual, a phone call, or in-person, this chapter prepares you to walk into any interview with confidence and clarity.

I begin with preparation because interviews are often won before they even start. That means researching the company thoroughly, its mission, values, culture, and the specifics of the role. You should know your own resume inside and out, ready to tell stories behind your experiences that demonstrate problem-solving, collaboration, leadership, and adaptability.

I explore the most common types of interview questions: behavioral, situational, and technical, and how to answer them using frameworks like STAR (Situation, Task, Action, Result). You'll learn how to talk about challenges honestly, successes humbly, and your potential enthusiastically. I also discuss preparing thoughtful questions for your interviewer, the kind that demonstrate curiosity, initiative, and a desire to grow within the company.

Virtual interviews get their own spotlight. In today's hybrid work environment, mastering virtual presence is essential, from camera angle and lighting to eliminating background distractions and maintaining eye contact on screen. However, the interview isn't over when the questions stop, the follow-up matters. A professional, personalized thank-you email sent within 24 hours reinforces your interest, appreciation, and attention to detail. This small step can set you apart in a crowded field.

Lastly, I address the aftermath; handling feedback, responding to rejections gracefully, and staying engaged, if you're placed in a talent pipeline. Every interview, whether it leads to an offer or not, is a learning experience and a step closer to your ideal role.

# CHAPTER 4
# INTERNSHIP AND JOB SEARCH STRATEGIES

The internship and job search process can feel like a whirlwind; applications, deadlines, rejections, interviews, networking events, it's enough to overwhelm even the most prepared student. But just like any mission that requires a successful launch, having a strategic approach can transform chaos into clarity and pressure into purpose.

This chapter is your guide to crafting a search strategy that is intentional, organized, and aligned with your goals, whether you're targeting a small startup, a mid-sized business, or a Fortune 500 organization. Each has its own culture, expectations, and pathways in. The key is to know where you're aiming before you take the shot.

Searching for an internship or entry-level job can feel overwhelming, especially in a competitive landscape filled with countless opportunities, varied application platforms, and evolving workplace expectations. But approaching the process with intention, focus, and strategy can shift your mindset from anxiety to purpose. This phase isn't just about landing any role, it's about discovering what aligns with your strengths, values, and long-term goals.

The first step begins with clarity rather than randomly applying to every open position; it's more effective to first reflect on what kind of experience you want. Do you thrive in structured corporate environments, or are you more drawn to the fast-paced, multi-tasking world of startups? Would you prefer to work for a company with a strong social mission, or are you looking for brand-name experience to strengthen your resume? Knowing these answers will help you filter opportunities that truly match your goals.

Once your direction is clear, building a focused list of target companies becomes more purposeful. This isn't about chasing big names alone, it's about identifying organizations whose culture, mission, and projects resonate with you. From there, the application process becomes a cycle of research, customization, and persistence. Every resume and cover letter you send should be tailored not just with your experience, but with language that speaks directly to the employer's needs. Generic applications get generic responses. Tailored applications show effort and intent, which can make a big difference in a crowded pool.

Equally important is tapping into networks as not all roles are advertised publicly, especially internships. Professors, advisors, alumni, and even family friends can be helpful sources for hidden opportunities. A simple, professional message of interest or a request for a short informational chat can open doors you didn't know existed. This is where platforms like LinkedIn become incredibly powerful, not just for applying, but for connecting with people already doing the kind of work you're aspiring to do.

As you navigate your search, treat it like a real commitment. Create a structured schedule with dedicated time for applying, networking, and following up. Keep track of where you've applied, when to expect responses, and when to send polite reminders. However, try not to get discouraged by rejections; they're part of the process. Every interview, even the ones that don't lead to an offer, helps sharpen your communication and build your resilience. Ultimately, the search process is not just about finding a role, it's about preparing for the role that will launch your career. Be intentional. Be open to feedback. Stay persistent, and remember you're not just looking for a job, you're designing your professional path.

## YOUR SEARCH EQUALS YOUR STORY IN THE MAKING

Every outreach email, every tailored application, every mock interview is preparing you not just for one job but for your long-term career. By approaching your search with strategy, patience, and adaptability, you're building the habits that will serve you well far beyond your first role.

Try not to rush the process, don't settle, prepare your materials, know what you're aiming for, and go after it with intention. You're not just applying for a job; you're preparing for your launch.

# CHAPTER 5
## INTERVIEWS IN ALL WORK SETTINGS
## REMOTE, HYBRID, AND ON-SITE

As the workplace evolves, so must the mindset of the modern intern or entry-level professional. Gone are the days when office life was confined to a cubicle, a 9-to-5 clock-in, and physical proximity to your team. Today, early-career employees are expected to thrive in three primary work environments: hybrid, remote, and on-site. Each demands unique skills; however, the common thread is your ability to adapt, stay productive, and maintain professional excellence, regardless of where or how you work.

## REMOTE: LEADING FROM BEHIND THE SCREEN

In a remote work setting, your independence becomes your superpower. Without the natural structure of an office, self-motivation, time discipline, and proactive communication are what set you apart. You may not have the luxury of tapping a coworker on the shoulder for help, but that doesn't mean you're alone. Thriving remotely means building digital bridges, checking in regularly with your manager, seeking clarity when needed, and being visible through your contributions, not just your presence in meetings.

Remote work also means mastering the art of digital professionalism. Your email tone, meeting presence, and response time become your brand. It's not just about logging hours; it's about delivering value without being micromanaged. When you're remote, initiative matters even more. You should never wait to be told what to do; instead, anticipate needs, stay organized, and make your progress visible.

## HYBRID: BALANCING BOTH WORLDS

Hybrid work environments require you to function seamlessly in two distinct realities: virtual and in-person. This setting can be both exciting and tricky. You might work from home three days a week and spend the other two at the office. That flexibility offers freedom, but it also calls for discipline and clarity. You must remain in sync with your team, even when you're not physically present. To thrive in a hybrid setting, organization is your best friend. Plan your in-office days with intentionality and schedule your collaborative meetings, brainstorming sessions, or face-to-face check-ins on those days. Use remote days for focused work, independent projects, or research. Remember, visibility isn't just about being seen, it's about being heard, engaged, and dependable across platforms.

In hybrid roles, it's also important to track what's happening in both spheres. Be alert to informal updates, hallway conversations, or decisions made during casual desk drop-ins. Ask colleagues or your supervisor to loop you in, and don't be afraid to confirm key takeaways from meetings, regardless of where you attended from. Being hybrid means being present, even when you're not physically there.

## ON-SITE: MAXIMIZING PHYSICAL PRESENCE

In on-site settings, your body language, energy, punctuality, and daily interactions carry more weight. When you're physically in the room, you get opportunities for impromptu conversations, real-time feedback, and mentorship that's harder to access remotely. Take advantage of these moments. Say hello. Ask thoughtful questions and offer to help. On-site environments also offer a natural rhythm start and end times, daily structure, and in-person accountability. But don't fall into the trap of thinking being present is the same as being productive. You still need to be proactive, engaged, and curious. Speak up in meetings, introduce yourself to other departments, and observe how leadership operates. The on-site environment is rich with learning moments, if you're paying attention.

On-site also teaches you the subtleties of workplace culture. How do teams collaborate? How do leaders lead? How are disagreements handled? These are things you feel when you're in the space, and they shape how you grow as a professional.

## MASTERING THE TRANSITION BETWEEN SETTINGS

For many early-career professionals, the challenge isn't just functioning in one setting, it's shifting between them. One week, you're on online calls in your bedroom. Next, you're expected to show up polished and poised in an office boardroom. That transition requires flexibility, self-awareness, and emotional intelligence. Here's the truth: the people who grow fastest in their careers are those who can succeed in any environment. They're consistent. They communicate clearly. They know how to read a room, whether physical or virtual. They know when to speak up and when to listen, and most importantly, they learn to be equally excellent and adaptable across every format.

You don't have to be perfect, but you do have to be intentional. Be mindful of how you show up in each space. Prepare. Plan. Learn from every mistake and carry those lessons into the next day, no matter where you're working from.

Your work environment doesn't define you. Your adaptability does!

# CHAPTER 6
# WORKPLACE ETIQUETTE, COMMUNICATION, AND CULTURE

Etiquette is more than just saying "please" and "thank you." It's the everyday behavior that signals respect, reliability, and emotional intelligence. From how you greet people in the morning to how you respond to emails, these details shape how others perceive you and often determine the opportunities you're trusted with.

Start with *punctuality*. Whether logging into a virtual meeting or arriving at an office, being on time shows that you value other people's schedules. Respect shared spaces, clean up after yourself in breakrooms or shared desks. Dress in a way that aligns with the company's culture, and when in doubt, aim for polished and neat. Etiquette also means being mindful of volume levels in open workspaces, listening more than speaking in meetings when you're new, and being polite, even when disagreements arise. These are the small things that build big trust.

## COMMUNICATION: THE LIFELINE OF SUCCESS

The way you communicate in the workplace will define how people respond to you. It's not about being the loudest voice in the room, it's about being *clear, concise, and thoughtful*. Effective communication involves knowing when to speak, how to listen, and selecting the most suitable method for conveying the message.

In professional settings, tone matters. Your emails, messages, and even slack replies leave an impression. Avoid sarcasm, overuse of emojis, or overly casual language, especially when interacting with supervisors or new colleagues. Instead, aim for professionalism with a friendly tone, respectful, warm, but straight to the point. Don't wait for others to come to you; ask for clarity when you need it. Confirm your understanding of instructions. Provide updates before you're asked, as good communicators don't just talk, they make others feel heard.

Also, recognize *non-verbal cues*. Eye contact in conversations, nodding when listening, or keeping your camera on during virtual calls sends the message: "I'm engaged." If your body language contradicts your words, it's your body that people will believe.

## CULTURE: READING THE ROOM (AND THE COMPANY)

Every organization has its own culture, a mix of values, behaviors, communication styles, and expectations. Some cultures are formal and process-driven, while others are collaborative and flexible. Understanding your company's culture is vital if you want to navigate it successfully and build meaningful professional relationships. Observe how leaders interact with their teams. Then ask yourself a few questions: Are emails formal or relaxed? Are meetings structured or free-flowing? How do people dress? What gets celebrated? These clues will help you understand what's expected and what's respected.

But culture is more than surface-level; it's also about how a company *treats people*, encourages feedback, manages conflict, and supports growth. As a new team member, take time to understand the core values behind the culture. Align yourself with them, not by imitation, but by finding how your own values can complement the environment.

Don't be afraid to ask questions:

- "What's the preferred way to communicate updates here?"
- "Is there anything I should know about how meetings are typically run?"

- "I'd love to understand more about the company culture. Any advice?"

Curiosity shows humility and a desire to integrate well.

## STAYING AUTHENTIC WHILE ADAPTING

One of the biggest fears early-career professionals have is losing their identity in the name of fitting in. Here's the truth. *You don't have to abandon who you are to be professional; you just need to be adaptable.* You can hold on to your values while adjusting to how you show up in different settings. It's about finding the balance between being yourself and being respectful of the environment you're in. You're not here to be a clone; you're here to contribute your uniqueness in a way that adds value to the team and reflects well on you.

Etiquette, communication, and culture are often what determine whether a manager says, "Let's bring them back for another project" or "They weren't quite ready." They might seem like soft skills, but they have hard consequences. Therefore, you need to show up with respect, speak with purpose, learn the environment, and remember that even as a new employee, your behavior sets the tone for how seriously others take you.

Now go make a lasting impression, one polished conversation at a time.

# CHAPTER 7
# TIME MANAGEMENT, PRIORITIZATION, AND MEETING DEADLINES

Time management isn't about being busy, it's about being intentional. Whether you're entering an internship, a new job, or balancing school and work, learning how to manage your time effectively is one of the most critical skills you can carry into any professional environment. This chapter explores how to structure your day, prioritize your work, and meet your deadlines without sacrificing your sanity. It's not just about doing more, it's about doing what matters most, consistently and well. Time isn't just money in the workplace; it's reputation, trust, and opportunity.

In the early stages of your career, how you manage your time becomes one of the most visible and critical aspects of your professional brand. Whether you're balancing multiple internships, transitioning into a full-time role, or navigating the remote-office blur, learning to manage your time with purpose and precision will set you apart. Managing time isn't about stuffing more into your calendar; it's about doing the right things at the right time and knowing when to say no.

Most new professionals underestimate how quickly time can disappear in a modern workplace. A day that begins with great intentions can vanish in a storm of messages, unexpected meetings, minor tasks, and inbox chaos. You sit down to work on a project, and the next thing you know, it's 3:45 p.m., and your best energy has been spent on things that weren't even on your list. Sound familiar? This is why intentional time management is crucial. Successful professionals plan their days before their days begin. That might mean setting aside 15 minutes each morning to review what needs to be done or creating a weekly plan that outlines top priorities. Some even use time-blocking, assigning chunks of time to specific types of work (deep focus, emails, meetings, etc.) to protect their energy and attention.

But time management only works when paired with prioritization. You can be incredibly productive at low-value tasks and still miss your goals. Prioritization means looking beyond what's urgent and identifying what's *important*. It's recognizing that not all tasks carry the same weight and sometimes, saying yes to one thing means saying no to something else. The most respected professionals are not those who say yes to everything, but rather those who know how to protect their time for tasks that move the needle.

If you're ever unsure about what matters most, ask yourself: What will have the biggest impact if completed today? What aligns with my team's goals? What will my manager or client care about most if I'm running short on time?

Deadlines are the heartbeat of the professional world. They're not just due dates, they're commitments. Delivering work on time tells your colleagues and supervisors that you're dependable, organized, and respectful of others' time. Missing deadlines, especially without notice, quickly erodes trust. In early roles and internships, being the person who "gets it done" is often what earns you more responsibilities, referrals, and return offers.

Of course, things don't always go as planned. That's life, and work. But here's the difference between a professional and an amateur. A professional sees the storm coming and communicates early. If you're falling behind, raise your hand, ask for support, and provide an updated timeline. Most managers will appreciate the honesty and problem-solving mindset far more than a last-minute excuse or silence until it's too late. Another overlooked but powerful aspect of managing deadlines is setting internal deadlines, which involve setting earlier personal target dates to account for review, unexpected changes, or additional tasks. If your final deliverable is due Friday, plan to finish it by Wednesday. That buffer can mean the difference between a rushed and refined approach, especially when feedback or emergencies arise.

Time management is also deeply affected by your environment. In remote and hybrid roles, where no one's looking over your shoulder, you must become your own project manager. That means turning off distractions, creating designated workspaces, and defining your workday with intention, even if you're working from a coffee shop or your bedroom. In on-site roles, it means learning how to protect your time from the office chatter, last-minute tasks, or non-stop meetings. Ultimately, mastering your time is about mastering yourself. It's about understanding your work rhythm, managing your energy, and respecting your commitments to yourself and others. You won't always get it right, and that's okay. But with each deadline met and each task prioritized with care, you'll build something invaluable: a reputation as someone people can count on. That's not just time well spent, that's career gold.

Your future depends on what you do with your time today.

# CHAPTER 8
# FEEDBACK, GROWTH, AND CONTINUOUS LEARNING

In the workplace, feedback is the compass that keeps you on course. It's the mirror that reflects how others perceive your work, communication, and presence. For many new professionals, feedback can feel intimidating, like a test you're afraid to fail. But those who learn to welcome and use it see their careers accelerate far beyond those who resist it.

Growth in any role is not about doing everything perfectly from day one. It's about staying open, learning continuously, and improving steadily. When you begin to see feedback not as criticism but as information you can use, you unlock one of the most valuable tools for long-term success.

## WHY FEEDBACK MATTERS

Feedback isn't just about fixing mistakes; it's about finding opportunities. In professional environments, even high performers receive regular feedback, because no one is above learning. Managers, colleagues, and even clients may share perspectives you can't see from your position. When you receive feedback, listen fully before reacting. It's natural to feel defensive or explain your side, but the most effective professionals know that their first job is to understand. Instead of thinking, *"They're saying I'm wrong,"* shift to *"They're showing me how to get better."* This shift transforms a potentially tense moment into an opportunity to enhance your skills and reputation.

## THE ART OF RECEIVING FEEDBACK

Taking feedback well is an underrated skill. If your supervisor tells you something needs improvement, avoid rushing to justify your actions. Instead, thank them, ask clarifying questions, and plan to address the points raised. This demonstrates maturity, accountability, and a willingness to learn. After a feedback conversation, take notes while the information is still fresh. Document what was said, why it matters, and the specific actions you'll take moving forward. This not only helps you improve but also demonstrates to your manager later that you listened to and acted on their input.

## THE COURAGE TO ASK FOR FEEDBACK

Waiting for feedback means you might only hear it when something goes wrong. Proactive professionals ask for it regularly, not just during performance reviews. By asking questions like, *"How do you think I handled that project?"* or *"Is there something I could be doing more effectively?"*, you show initiative and an investment in your own growth. The key is to create a feedback-friendly relationship with your colleagues and supervisors. When they know you welcome input, they're more likely to offer guidance that helps you avoid problems before they arise.

## TURNING FEEDBACK INTO ACTION

Receiving feedback is just the first step. The real power comes when you take what you've learned and apply it. Small changes made consistently can transform the way you work. If you're told your reports are too long, practice summarizing key points. If your presentations feel rushed, rehearse with a timer. The goal isn't perfection, it's progress. Every adjustment you make builds your skill set and your professional credibility.

## GROWTH IS A MINDSET, NOT A MILESTONE

True growth is ongoing. It's not about reaching a destination but about staying open to learning in every stage of your career. The moment you believe you have nothing left to learn, you start to limit your potential. Read industry articles, attend workshops, join webinars, and engage with professional networks. Learn from colleagues in different roles. Observe how experienced team members handle challenges. Even outside of work, every interaction can teach you something about communication, problem-solving, or leadership.

## CONTINUOUS LEARNING IN ACTION

In today's fast-paced world, skills can become outdated in a matter of months. Continuous learning keeps you relevant. For example, if your industry adopts a new software tool, don't wait for formal training; seek tutorials, practice independently, and share what you learn with your team. This adaptability makes you invaluable. Continuous learning is also about self-awareness, knowing your strengths, and identifying areas where you need growth. Pair this with regular reflection: ask yourself every month, *"What new skills have I developed? What challenges did I overcome? Where can I improve next?"*

Feedback, growth, and continuous learning form a cycle: you receive input, act on it, improve, and invite more input. Over time, this loop builds your confidence, competence, and career resilience. You'll find that people begin to see you as someone who doesn't just work hard but someone who learns fast and adapts even faster. Remember: feedback is not a personal attack, it's a gift. Growth is not about knowing everything; it's about staying curious. Continuous learning isn't a side activity; it's the engine that drives your career forward.

Every piece of feedback is a stepping stone, not a stumbling block.

# CHAPTER 9

# NAVIGATING DIFFICULT MOMENTS AND PROFESSIONAL BOUNDARIES

No matter how skilled, prepared, or positive you are, difficult moments in the workplace will happen. A project will fall apart, a deadline will be missed, a coworker will rub you the wrong way, or a manager will misunderstand your intentions. What separates professionals who thrive from those who crumble is not whether they face challenges, but how they respond to them. These moments can be stressful, but they also present opportunities to demonstrate your professionalism, resilience, and emotional intelligence. When handled well, these moments can strengthen relationships, improve your credibility, and accelerate your growth.

## THE CALM IN THE STORM

The first rule when navigating challenges is simple: stay calm, even if the situation feels urgent or unfair. Emotional reactions, such as snapping back in a meeting, sending a heated email, or shutting down entirely, can damage your professional image in seconds. In contrast, a calm demeanor invites problem-solving and keeps conversations productive. Instead, pause before responding. Take a breath, gather your thoughts, and focus on what you *want* to achieve from the interaction. This doesn't mean suppressing your feelings; it means directing them in a way that leads to a constructive outcome. Remaining composed doesn't mean ignoring your feelings; it means managing them so they don't control the outcome. The professionals who rise in their careers are often the ones who can remain steady when others are losing their cool.

## ADDRESSING CONFLICT CONSTRUCTIVELY

Workplace disagreements are inevitable, but they don't have to be destructive. Whether it's a misunderstanding about responsibilities, a clash in communication styles, or tension over differing ideas, the key is to address the issue early and respectfully. Seek to understand before you try to be understood. Instead of starting with accusations ("You never listen"), start with observations and questions ("I noticed we had different approaches, can we talk about what's working and what's not?"). This shifts the conversation from a personal attack to a shared problem-solving moment. Conflict is not inherently negative; it can spark innovation and clarify misunderstandings if handled correctly. When issues arise, the goal is not to "win" but to find a resolution that works for everyone involved. This approach maintains relationships and often leads to solutions that neither side considered initially.

## BOUNDARIES: YOUR PROFESSIONAL GUARDRAILS

Boundaries are not about being difficult, they're about protecting your well-being and productivity. Without them, you risk burnout, resentment, and even a loss of respect from colleagues. Setting boundaries can mean clarifying your working hours, defining your scope of responsibilities, or learning to say "no" when requests pull you away from your priorities. Boundaries also apply to interpersonal behavior, such as refusing to engage in gossip, declining to share overly personal details at work, or making it clear that disrespectful communication is not acceptable. When you set boundaries early and stick to them, you train others to respect both your time and your role. Boundaries safeguard both your effectiveness and your well-being. Without them, you risk overextending yourself, taking on tasks outside your scope, or becoming a go-to for non-urgent interruptions that derail your productivity. These limits help maintain a professional atmosphere and signal that you take your work seriously.

## COMMUNICATING YOUR BOUNDARIES EFFECTIVELY

The way you communicate your boundaries determines how they're received. Be polite, clear, and consistent. For example, instead of saying, "I'm too busy for that," you might say, "I'm working on a deadline right now, but I can take a look after lunch." This acknowledges the request without sacrificing your focus. If a colleague or manager repeatedly crosses your boundaries, address the issue directly and respectfully. Often, people don't even realize they've overstepped. Clear communication keeps resentment from building and relationships from deteriorating, consistency matters. If you enforce a boundary one day but ignore it the next, others may become confused about your limits. The more consistently you uphold your boundaries, the more naturally others will respect them.

## KNOWING WHEN TO ESCALATE

Sometimes, a difficult moment exceeds what you can handle on your own, such as harassment, unethical requests, or repeated disrespect. In these cases, the professional thing to do is to escalate the matter through the proper channels, such as HR or a trusted leader. When escalating, keep your documentation factual and specific, avoiding emotional language that could dilute the seriousness of the concern. Reference company policies where relevant and follow internal procedures closely. Far from being "troublemaking," escalation is a way of protecting yourself and maintaining the integrity of the workplace.

## THE ROLE OF EMOTIONAL INTELLIGENCE

Professional boundaries and difficult moments are easier to navigate when you understand emotional intelligence (EQ). EQ involves recognizing your emotions, understanding the emotions of others, and managing both effectively. In tense situations, a high EQ enables you to read the room, choose your words carefully, and adjust your approach according to the other person's communication style. This skill can mean the difference between a disagreement that escalates and one that resolves quickly. Emotional intelligence (EQ) is at the heart of navigating workplace challenges and maintaining boundaries. For example, when delivering critical feedback, a high-EQ approach ensures your tone is constructive rather than accusatory. When receiving feedback, it helps you listen without defensiveness, even if the message is hard to hear. This adaptability fosters trust and maintains a professional tone, even in emotionally charged situations.

## GROWTH THROUGH CHALLENGES

Every setback offers a learning opportunity if you take the time to reflect. After a difficult moment, ask yourself: What triggered the problem? How did I contribute to the outcome, positively or negatively? What would I handle differently next time? This self-reflection builds resilience, sharpens decision-making skills, and enhances your ability to anticipate and prevent future issues. Over time, you'll find that the situations that once rattled you become easier to navigate.

## PROTECTING YOUR REPUTATION IN HARD TIMES

People remember how you behave when things go wrong. If you handle pressure with integrity, fairness, and composure, you build trust that lasts. Colleagues will know they can rely on you in high-stakes situations, which often leads to more responsibility and opportunities. Professional boundaries and effective handling of difficult moments are not about building walls, they're about building respect. In the long run, respect is one of the most valuable assets in any career. Your reputation is built over years but can be damaged in minutes. Handling challenges with grace and integrity demonstrates reliability and leadership potential. Treating everyone with respect, even in the most difficult circumstances, positions you as someone worth trusting with greater responsibilities and opportunities.

Your reaction in tough times defines your reputation more than your reaction in easy ones.

# CHAPTER 10
# FINAL LAUNCH TIPS: THRIVING BEYOND DAY ONE

The start of a new job or internship is a milestone, but it's not the finish line; it's the starting block. Once the initial excitement fades, what matters most is how you consistently show up, contribute, and grow. The weeks and months after your launch will shape your reputation, relationships, and career trajectory. Your first day in a new role might be full of excitement, nerves, and information overload. However, thriving in your internship or early career extends far beyond the initial handshake and onboarding schedule. Success comes from consistently showing up, being adaptable, and finding ways to add value, all while learning and growing. These final tips are designed to help you not only survive but thrive in your first professional chapter.

## BE CURIOUS: ASK QUESTIONS WITHOUT HESITATION

One of the most underrated traits in any professional setting is genuine curiosity. Too many people fear that asking questions will make them look inexperienced. The opposite is true; thoughtful questions show that you're engaged, eager to understand the bigger picture, and willing to learn. The best time to ask questions is early on, when expectations are still being established and your role is still being defined. Questions about processes, team priorities, and preferred communication methods help you avoid mistakes later. If you're unsure about a task, confirm the details rather than making assumptions that could create more work for yourself and others.

Not all questions need to be about "how to do something." Some of the most valuable ones are about "why we do it this way" or "what the end goal is." These questions deepen your understanding of your work's impact and help you connect individual tasks to larger business objectives. Over time, this insight enables you to become more strategic, not just operational. This shows that you're proactive and respectful of their time. Even after you understand the basics of your role, learning should never stop, as workplaces are dynamic and constantly evolving, with new tools, projects, and expectations emerging all the time. By treating each task as an opportunity to deepen your knowledge, you not only strengthen your own skills but also demonstrate your value to the organization. Whether it's attending training sessions, seeking mentorship, or exploring industry trends, maintaining curiosity keeps you ahead of the curve and positions you as a proactive, engaged professional.

*Tip:* *Keep a running list of questions as they come to mind and ask them in batches during check-ins with your supervisor.*

## STAY ENGAGED, VISIBLE, AND BUILD RELATIONSHIPS INTENTIONALLY

The quiet fade into the background is one of the easiest traps to fall into after your first few weeks. You may be aware of your responsibilities and feel comfortable with your tasks, but visibility is crucial in any work environment. This doesn't mean constant self-promotion; it means showing that you're present, engaged, and committed. Participate in team discussions, volunteer for projects that challenge your skills, and keep your manager informed of your progress without being prompted. In remote or hybrid settings, this visibility can come from being active in group chats, contributing during virtual meetings, or sharing updates on collaborative tools. The goal is to be remembered for your contributions, not overlooked because you quietly did your work in the corner.

Your network inside the organization can be just as important as your actual performance. Relationships foster trust, open doors to mentorship, and provide allies who can advocate for you when opportunities arise. This doesn't mean trying to be everyone's best friend. It means engaging with people respectfully, showing genuine interest in their work, and identifying opportunities for collaboration. A short conversation in the breakroom, a follow-up email after a meeting, or a quick message to thank someone for their help all add up. In remote settings, where casual hallway interactions are not common, you may need to be more intentional. Schedule virtual coffee chats, attend optional networking calls, and find shared-interest groups within the company. Relationships built in the early stages can make it easier to navigate challenges later.

Your professional network within the organization is vital. Strong relationships foster trust, provide support, and create opportunities for collaboration. Connecting with colleagues across teams, checking in with mentors, and participating in social or professional events helps you understand the broader context of the organization while establishing allies who can advocate for you in the future. Even small interactions, like expressing appreciation for someone's help or engaging in meaningful conversations, strengthen your presence and demonstrate your investment in the team's success.

## SEEK FEEDBACK EARLY AND OFTEN

Waiting until your annual review to know how you're doing is a missed opportunity. Regular feedback keeps you aligned with expectations and helps you adjust before small issues become big problems. After completing a major task or project, ask for specific input: "What worked well, and what could I improve next time?" This not only shows humility but also signals that you're committed to growth. Remember, feedback is not criticism; it's information that helps you get better. The more comfortable you get with receiving feedback, the faster you'll improve. And by acting on that feedback, you demonstrate adaptability, one of the most valued traits in any workplace.

Standing out requires more than completing your assigned tasks. Observing processes, identifying potential improvements, and contributing ideas shows initiative and commitment. By volunteering for challenging projects or offering support during busy periods, you demonstrate a proactive mindset. These actions convey reliability, resourcefulness, and leadership potential, which are noticed by managers and colleagues alike.

## STAY FLEXIBLE, ADAPT TO CHANGE

The only constant in any career is change. Projects shift, priorities get redefined, and teams reorganize. Those who cling to "the way it's always been" often struggle to stay relevant.

Flexibility is a skill that can be strengthened by treating changes as challenges rather than obstacles. When faced with a shift, ask clarifying questions ("What's the new priority?" "How will this impact deadlines?") and think about how you can best support the new direction. Adaptable employees aren't just survivors; they often become the go-to people when leadership needs problem-solvers.

Workplaces are rarely static; projects shift, priorities evolve, and new challenges emerge. Embracing change rather than resisting it allows you to stay effective and relevant. By viewing adjustments as opportunities to learn and improve, you enhance your adaptability, a skill highly valued in any professional setting. Asking clarifying questions, staying positive, and adjusting your approach when needed ensure that you can navigate transitions smoothly.

## INVEST IN CONTINUOUS LEARNING

Your degree or experience got you in the door, but ongoing learning will keep you moving forward. This doesn't always mean formal training; it could be shadowing a senior colleague, exploring an internal knowledge base, or using downtime to study industry trends. Stay curious about your field, your company, and your role. Seek out resources, attend workshops, and leverage internal learning platforms, if they're available. By consistently expanding your knowledge, you're also preparing yourself for future roles and responsibilities. Clear and confident communication builds credibility and prevents misunderstandings. Being deliberate in how you articulate ideas, provide updates, or ask questions shows professionalism.

Following up on discussions, actively listening to colleagues, and tailoring your communication style to your audience, whether peers, supervisors, or executives, establishes you as a dependable and approachable individual. Acknowledging achievements boosts confidence and provides tangible evidence of your contributions. Whether completing projects, improving processes, or receiving positive feedback, celebrating these moments reinforces motivation. Equally important is reflecting on challenges and mistakes as learning opportunities, allowing you to refine your skills and approach without discouragement.

## MAINTAIN YOUR PROFESSIONAL STANDARDS

As you grow comfortable in your role, it's tempting to loosen the standards you held in the early days; arriving right on time becomes arriving a little late, or double-checking your work becomes optional. However, consistency is key to long-term credibility. Continue to meet deadlines, keep commitments, and present yourself with the same professionalism you showed when making your first impression. Over time, people notice when someone's reliability endures beyond the probationary period, and that's a reputation worth holding on to. Document your achievements, whether it's completing a project ahead of schedule, improving a process, or receiving positive feedback. These moments not only boost confidence but also serve as great talking points in performance reviews or future job interviews.

At the same time, reflect on mistakes without self-criticism. Every misstep is a lesson that can sharpen your professional skills. Maintaining high performance requires attention to your energy levels. Knowing when you are most productive, taking brief restorative breaks, and setting boundaries between work and personal life ensures sustained focus and effectiveness. Energy management enables you to bring your best self to every task, thereby enhancing both the quality of your work and your professional presence.

## FINAL WORD: KEEP THE LAUNCH MINDSET ALIVE

The "Day One energy" you felt at the start, curiosity, enthusiasm, attentiveness, isn't just for the first week. If you can keep that mindset alive, you'll continue to stand out long after your new-hire status fades. Ask questions, seek understanding, build relationships, and remain open to new growth opportunities. Success beyond day one is about more than doing the job; it's about becoming someone your team can rely on, trust, and learn from. If you can achieve that, you're not just surviving in your role, you're thriving.

Thriving beyond day one is about adopting habits that reinforce growth, engagement, and professional resilience. By maintaining a learning mindset, building meaningful relationships, contributing beyond expectations, adapting to change, communicating effectively, asking thoughtful questions, managing your energy, and reflecting on both successes and lessons, you lay the foundation for a fulfilling and impactful career. Every action, challenge, and achievement builds toward the professional you aspire to become.

Your first day may open the door, but your long-term success depends on how you walk through it every day after.

# ABOUT THE AUTHOR

Kaydian Williams is a Human Resources professional, mentor, and author committed to helping students and emerging professionals navigate the transition from education to career with confidence and clarity. Drawing from her extensive experience, she has dedicated her work to bridging the gap between academic preparation and real-world success.

Her approach is both practical and motivational, offering strategies that empower readers to take ownership of their career journeys. Whether preparing resumes and cover letters, navigating interviews in hybrid or remote settings, or building strong workplace relationships, Kaydian emphasizes actionable steps that create real momentum. She believes that confidence is not built overnight but developed through preparation, intentional choices, and a willingness to learn and grow.

In her book, *Launchpad: A Real-World Guide to Internships and Entry-Level Success*, Kaydian distills her expertise into a supportive roadmap designed to help readers succeed from day one and beyond. Her writing reflects a commitment to excellence, encouragement, and the belief that every individual has the potential to contribute meaningfully in their chosen path.

Kaydian continues to dedicate her time to mentorship, professional development, and creating resources that inspire and guide others toward success. Her mission is clear: to help students and early professionals not just find opportunities but thrive in them, transforming uncertainty into confidence and potential into achievement.

Connect with Kaydian Williams for speaking engagements, mentorship, and career development resources:

**Email**: authenticimpact.25@gmail.com
**Social Media:** LinkedIn- Kaydian Williams
www.linkedin.com/in/kaydian-williams-peoplefirst

www.ingramcontent.com/pod-product-compliance
Lightning Source LLC
Chambersburg PA
CBHW051245120626
46547CB00014B/1809